INTRODUCTION

What do you want?

This may be a question that you ask yourself a lot, or maybe you haven't really thought about it. What do any of us really want? Likely answers are: money, a loving relationship, a fabulous body or good health - maybe all of these things and more! When I asked myself that very same question some time ago, I very quickly landed upon the 'money' solution. Of course, money would make me happy - it would solve all of my problems! I then asked myself what I would do if I had plenty (and I mean, PLENTY) of money and started to think of what I would do with it. I enjoyed planning all the things I could have and all the things I could do and I revelled in how it would make me feel - and it felt pretty good! So, obviously, that was my answer to the question: it was money that I wanted. Money would make me happy.

However, then I dug a bit deeper and challenged myself further - what if I had £10,000,000 in the bank, but I wasn't allowed to spend any of it? Obviously, my life would be no better than it already was and I would be no happier. If, on the other hand, I were allowed to spend the money, my lifestyle would change: I would have lots more time to do the things that make my heart sing and I would not have to worry about money any more because I would feel financially safe and free. So, in reality, it is those feelings of safety and freedom that my rich lifestyle would afford me that would make me truly happy, not the actual money itself.

This realisation led me to the idea that ultimately, that is what we all want - to be happy. Yes, having lots of money is a fantastic tool to achieving safety, freedom and happiness, in that it enables

1

us to live our lives in the way we choose, but it is the feelings created by that lifestyle that ultimately cause our happiness. And that's the same for anything we want: if we desire a loving relationship, it's because we know it will make us happy; if we desire a fabulous body, it's because we know it will make us happy. We often wish for 'things' because we think they will make us happy. But if it's ultimately happiness that we want, what if we could bypass getting all those 'things' and just be happy with exactly what we have? Would we still feel we wanted that money, that relationship or that body?

I've wrestled with this idea for a while. There are, naturally, things that I want and strive for (that is the nature of humanity, after all) and I have, as much as anyone else has, held the belief that I can't be truly happy until I possess those 'things'. But what if we could somehow feel happier without those 'things'? How could we make that happen? Can we become happier with what we already have?

Don't worry, this is not a book that will tell you to 'just be grateful' for what you have, which will then magically make you happy. I wrote this book because I want to help you to discover 'The Power of Happy' for yourself, as I have. In fact, I wish I had read this book a few years ago, as I know it would have helped me immensely and that is exactly what I want to do for you. This book contains a set of simple strategies that I have personally used and which have changed my life immensely - little effort for big results! I hope you don't mind the accompanying anecdotes, which I have included in the hope they will enable you to put the strategies into some sort of context and give them more meaning - and also because I just love to tell a story.

I hardly recognise myself now, compared to how I used to be just a couple of short years ago. I was miserable. I felt stressed and resentful towards everyone. I was suspicious of everyone and everything. I looked for the negative in every situation in order to 'protect' myself from it. And the more I looked for the negatives, the more I found and the more miserable I became. It was a self-perpetuating negative cycle.

Then one day (I don't even remember what day it was or why it was different from any other day), I knew something had to change, and fortunately, I had the wisdom to realise that there was nothing I could change - except me. I had to change. I was driving myself to distraction hating the world! That isn't the person I wanted to be! I remember suddenly having a vision of myself on my death bed, looking back and contemplating my life. I could not bear to accept that how I was feeling, and the way I was living my life, was how I would remember myself, and even more importantly, that that is how my family would remember me! I suddenly felt ashamed, as though I was wasting my life with all this negativity. I knew I had to do something if I wanted my life to get better - I had to try to be a better person, I had to try to be happier. So I did! It was actually really simple - I just needed to want to do it.

I started immediately by just trying to see the good things I had in my life (we all have them, we just sometimes overlook them) and to consciously ignore the bad things (yes, I believed I had more than my fair share of those) and things began to change very rapidly. I very quickly understood that I had the power within me to feel better, to feel happier. I didn't need to change anything about my circumstances, I just needed to see the good. I stopped blaming others for how I was feeling and took responsibility for myself. I soon became quite addicted to seeing positive in everything around me - and it felt great. It became like a fun game to play and I won every time. I was so proud myself. Of course, there were things about my life that weren't right for me and that I have since changed (in a positive, enlightened way), but I needed to become a more positive, happy person in order to see things as they truly were, not through my mud-tinted spectacles which made it appear as though everything was wrong.

Hopefully, you're now thinking that you're going to enjoy this book and that you'll become happier through reading it and applying these simple strategies. This is certainly true, but there is something even more exciting that will happen to you. Through reading this book and becoming more happy - a great result in itself - you will also come to understand the power that happiness has to bring unexpectedly wonderful things into your life. Happiness is power. Happiness is not just an end in itself, but a tool. When you grow your happiness, you grow your power. By making just one small change in your life, you will be a bit more happy, which gives you the power to make another change, causing more happiness and more power and before you know it, your happiness has grown immensely and your life has improved unimaginably.

It starts with one small change - and you can make that change today. Tomorrow you will reap the rewards and, step by step, day by day, this will lead you to a lifetime of happiness.

SAY 'THANK YOU'

To say that I put my heart and soul into looking after my two children, is an understatement. While they were young, it felt as though every fibre of my being had only one purpose – to be the best mum I could be and make sure they had the very best start in their lives, in order for them to become the independent, confident and successful adults we, as parents, want them to be. The fear that I would look back and think, "We should have done a better job," filled me with dread and guilt on a daily basis. I remember reading that what a child experiences in the first six years of life has a huge impact on shaping the rest of his or her life. Six years! Six short years! Or six long years, when you're immersed in that constant questioning and guilt that you might not be doing it right - and that you won't discover until it is too late! We have two children, three years apart, so those early 'I am responsible for shaping the rest of your life' years went on for nine years. No wonder I was a nervous wreck!

However, now that my children are older, I sometimes allow myself the luxury of sitting back and adopting a more watchful role - watching to see if they have actually turned out how I'd hoped, watching for any clues that we might just have got something right. Thankfully, I love what I see, and everyday I see them developing further into amazing individuals, making genius decisions and choosing their own pathways; they are certainly not just the product of what we put into them. I know we still have a great deal of influence over them, and I never take this for granted, humbly accepting it as part of the privilege of being a parent. As much as I have high expectations of and for my children, I expect far more of myself as their mum.

Showing gratitude and appreciation has been highly researched and there is evidence to show it to be one of the best things you can do to increase happiness. It is the opposite of anger/frustration/feelings of lack and it is impossible to feel these negative thoughts whilst you are feeling gratitude. Thinking about my children always makes me feel grateful - grateful that they are well-rounded, ambitious, well-mannered, excitable, vivacious individuals who have a love for life - and ultimately, grateful that we have them in our lives. I feel so excited when I think of what the future could hold for them, and appreciate those 'moments' we share, whether it is a conversation at the dinner table or an insightful one-to-one chat at bedtime. They just make my heart sing and I now recognise that feeling as pure love and gratitude.

Once I'd become really good at not just feeling this gratitude, but recognising it as such, it made me notice all the other things in my life for which I am grateful. Some things are obvious and spring to mind immediately, but I also tend to spend much of each day noticing things which I previously wouldn't have - simple things that make me smile, like a dog trotting happily along with its owner, the flowers blooming on a front garden that I drive past, someone talking and laughing with a friend in the street. There are so many things to feel grateful for, the trick is to notice and appreciate them. I challenge you to see how many you can spot in the next hour - and how many times you smile. So simple, yet so powerful!

WHO ARE YOU? WHO DO YOU WANT TO BE?

Spend some time getting to know yourself – and I mean really getting to know yourself by digging deep! Try this: write down 10 personal characteristics which define you. Don't spend a long time doing this – just write down the first 10 things that come into your head – both positive and negative. Now have another look at that list. If you asked a close friend or relative to write a list about you, would the lists be the same? Probably not! Are there any things on the list that you're not sure about, now that you've had the chance to review it? Does the list accurately describe who you are? Spend a bit of time editing it. Cross out those characteristics you can't actually justify after analysing them more closely, and add any others that pop into your head. If you're not sure about any of the characteristics and whether they accurately describe you, try to think of specific examples and how often you behave in that way.

Once you have a final list, mark each characteristic with a tick or a cross, depending on whether or not you like that characteristic. For those you do like (e.g. generous, accepting), consider how you could enhance them even further. You need to know (although you may not yet believe it) that you are capable of changing any of your characteristics - you simply need the desire to do it. Rather than deleting a negative characteristic from your personality, you need to replace it with a positive one. So, just cross out the negative trait from your list and write a new, positive one next to it instead. Like habits, the way to stop a bad one, is to replace it with a good one, and characteristics are simply habits we have formed over time that have shaped our personality. We created them for ourselves and we can change them. By the time you've finished this exercise, you'll have a final list of 10 characteristics, all positive. Read that list again to yourself. While you do so, imagine having each characteristic in turn; imagine doing things on a daily basis that will demonstrate to you and the whole world that this is one of the characteristics that shape the person you are. Allow yourself to feel proud of being that person!

I'll repeat again, at this point, that you are able to change any of your characteristics, if you want to. This list will be a valuable tool in helping you to become the person you want to be. Look at your list every day and visualise yourself doing things to reinforce those characteristics. If you do this, you won't be able to help but do those things and become that person. If you can imagine it, you can do it. Bryan Tracy (author of 'Eat That Frog' - a brilliant read!) says that if you write down your goals every day, you will automatically do things which make them become real. Shawn Achor (in 'Before Happiness' - another great read!) explains it in a slightly different way - he says that what you focus on, is where you will end up. So, focus on who you want to be, and that is who you will become!

GOAL!

This section follows quite nicely from the last. Setting yourself personal goals to achieve, both long-term and short-term can have a very powerful impact on your life, particularly if you write them down. As I mentioned in the last section, some experts suggest writing your goals everyday, whilst others say you should write them once and then read them every day. I used both of these methods when I first started to set goals for myself, but nowadays, they are so embedded in who I am, I feel I don't need to keep writing or reading them - but I do think about them everyday. My goals are also quite fluid in that they change as my life improves and develops. I like to spend a bit of time each morning thinking about my goals and considering whether they are still relevant to my future life or whether new goals are now more relevant or enticing. It may be useful to separate your goals into different areas and think of one or more for each of these areas e.g. family, career, money, health, spirituality. You may want to order your goals by priority or time – it may be necessary to achieve a family goal before you can work on a career goal. Remember, these are your goals so set them as you will.

You can use affirmations in conjunction with your goals to 'tell' yourself you have already achieved them and to feel grateful for this. It tricks the subconscious mind into believing that you truly have already achieved these goals and it makes them a reality for you - especially if you repeat your affirmations regularly, as repetition is a great way to reprogram the subconscious mind. For instance, if you tell yourself over and over that you are confident, your subconscious mind starts to believe it and will actually make you feel confident throughout your day. It helps if you can picture yourself feeling confident too, and truly believing it, rather than just saying it. The simple act of repeating your affirmations to yourself in this way will really help them to come true. For instance, I used to say regularly say to myself, "I am happy and confident." When I first started to say this affirmation, I didn't feel particularly happy or confident, but within a few weeks I suddenly noticed that I really did feel these things. I started to believe that I was happy and confident and, if I believed it, it must be true! I had made it true! Had I spent my time telling myself that I was lonely and scared, guess what would have happened? Exactly – these things would have then become my reality.

I think the most difficult part of creating personal affirmations is choosing them. Firstly, it can seem overwhelming to choose just one or two things to improve in your life, especially if you feel like you have so many things you want to change. But I would certainly recommend choosing so few, so you can really focus on improving those – it gives them more importance and they become true much more quickly. Once you feel as though you have made some headway with these things and that you can see how your life has changed and improved, you will feel more confident choosing further goals to aim for. Maybe the next couple of goals could be more challenging! If there is a goal which seems more difficult to achieve or that you feel you may need to spend more time and energy in changing, it may be best to choose just this one goal, to really give it the emphasis and energy it needs and deserves.

SWITCH NEGATIVE TO POSITIVE

We all do it – we're programmed to do it! We wake up thinking about the day ahead and imagine all the things that could go wrong, or that will cause us stress. During my 'darker days', I used to think that if I'd have known at the start of the day what the day ahead would be like, I'd just have stayed in bed! And when we make predictions about what the day ahead has in store for us, it can seem overwhelming and even impossible! It's not our fault we feel like this – it's about survival.

Back in the days when we were cavemen and cavewomen, we were always on high alert for things around us that could kill us. It was so easy to be killed in those days - and pretty hard to stay alive! In fact, the reason we're all here today is due to the skills of our ancestors in being able to stay alive - we are born and bred survivors. Yay us! But, unfortunately, those skills that were once so useful to us, can now work against us in modern society. Yes, we do have stresses to deal with in our lives, but very few of these now cause the difference between life and death. It's just that our brains haven't yet caught up with that fact. We tend to over-dramatise things because our instinct is survival and we can trace all our worries and concerns back to our basic need to stay alive. Consider a few of the types of things we worry about:

* Money - worst case scenario: we will have no money to feed ourselves or our families and we will die and our blood-line will die with us.

* Relationships - worst case scenario: we will not find a mate and our blood-line will die when we die.

* Our appearance - worst case scenario: we will not attract a mate and our blood-line will die when we die.

Yes, I know these concerns seem ridiculous when broken down in this way, but to our undeveloped caveman/woman brain, these threats are real. Kind of puts the whole worrying thing in perspective, doesn't it? It also allows us to forgive ourselves for reacting in this way, knowing it's not our fault. The good news is that now we know why we react in this way, and can rationalise it, we can change it!

There are many ways we can change our negative thoughts (worries) into positives. One easy strategy to use is to simply recognise that a negative thought has entered your head and say 'no' to it, before replacing it with a positive thought instead. For example, if I catch myself imagining that in a work meeting I will be asked awkward, embarrassing questions that I cannot answer, making me feel like a complete failure, I say 'no' to myself and then imagine being asked questions that I can answer easily and actually make me appear and feel rather clever. The second option is so much nicer - and it's our choice which scenario we pick.

Another strategy (and this is one of my favourites because it's such good fun!) is ridiculing the negative feeling. If I catch myself thinking negatively about something that may happen (and experience has taught me that nothing is ever as bad as I can imagine it to be), I simply exaggerate the situation until it appears ridiculous. For example, if I am thinking about the meeting I will be having with my boss later that day and I start to imagine that he will ask me questions that I can't answer, or that he will catch me out by asking me for something that I haven't done and should have, I simply exaggerate the situation in my mind to make it seem ludicrous. This could be by imagining bizarre things such as my boss turning into a demon-possessed monster, complete with spinning head and green vomit. He might pick me up, spin me round above his head and throw me at the wall. Now, I know this is highly unlikely to happen and it even makes me chuckle to myself, thus making my original worry seem ridiculous too. Go on, try it - it's such great fun and it really works!

Remember, nothing can make us feel bad unless we let it! Our thoughts and feelings are not there to control us; we control them (even though this might not seem true at times!) and with practice, you will certainly come to see and believe this.

LET THE WORLD BE YOUR TEACHER

All too often, we find we are too busy to listen. We go about our lives being busy and doing things the ways we do things, because that's the way we do things and there isn't really time to rethink how we do them. Our subconscious mind controls our thoughts and actions 95% of the time, leaving only 5% of our time for the conscious mind to consider the choices we make rationally and make changes if necessary. That's pretty scary, especially if our subconscious mind is programmed to react negatively! So, I guess we're stuck with those subconscious decisions we make taking control of the majority of our lives? Not at all! If you could do something in a different way that would save you time or make you feel happier, isn't it worth taking the time to consider this consciously?

I'm not saying that you have to re-evaluate your whole belief system and start from scratch, but you can train yourself to become more aware of what others say, how they describe how they run their lives and always be open to considering, 'Is that way better than mine?' or "That doesn't sound very self-supportive - but do I also do that?' People love giving advice – everywhere you go, people are giving others the benefit of their wisdom and, sometimes, you can pick up some really valuable snippets of information about how to make your own life run smoother, if you are prepared to listen and consider what others are saying.

It is really important here to be open-minded and not to just blindly accept what others say and think that they must be right because they sound confident. Conversely, don't just assume that they must be wrong because you don't want to be told what to do and that you think you know better. Be humble, but not naïve. Consider your own beliefs and ideas thoughtfully. Is the idea worth trying out? Is it possible that it could work in your life? If not, is there some nugget of value in what is being suggested that could help you?

It may be that you overhear a conversation at the park or supermarket (I'm always listening to other people's conversations and I justify that by thinking that if people are speaking loudly enough to be heard by a perfect stranger – me – then the conversation can't be that private). If you can gain a snippet of information that helps to make something better in your life, then go ahead and steal it! What I'm saying is, listen out for others' ideas, be open to how they might help you and try them out if they seem useful. Who knows what you may discover! And if you still feel uneasy listening into other people's conversations, think about how that person would feel if they knew they had helped you to improve your life in some say. They'd probably be dead chuffed! You could even tell them if you wanted to, to pass on the good feelings.

To take this idea to the extreme - being more open-minded and listening to others - I recently bought a dog. No, I didn't just rush out and buy one (I'm certainly not that impulsive or irresponsible) but after hearing people at work talking about how they'd take their dogs on lovely long walks and how it made them reconnect with nature and take time out from their hectic schedules just to spend time walking the dog, I thought I'd get myself some of that joy! My family couldn't believe it - I'd always said we couldn't get a dog because we were all too busy and didn't have time etc. But I can honestly say it is one of the best things I have ever done! Having our cockapoo, Billy, has made me slow down and rather than feeling I don't have time to take him for walks, I love making time for this and I now have a much deeper appreciation for the simpler things in life. Now, I have an excuse to walk in the woods, to lie on the grass looking up at the clouds, to paddle in the river, to take in the views on our daily walks - not that anyone should feel the need to find an excuse to do this, but, in reality, we're unlikely to see this as a priority.

The best thing of all about having a dog is the constant stream of unconditional love between us. No matter how I am feeling, giving him a cuddle and a stroke is just so soothing and fulfilling. I cannot recommend it highly enough. There is just so much more love in my life now that I have him - and that can't be a bad thing! And I'd never have considered buying a dog had I not 'listened' to what others were saying. I hope Billy knows how lucky he is!

SOUL APPLES

What is it about an apple? It has become a symbol of health. Just looking at a picture of an apple makes my mouth water. I used to have an obsession with apples, eating as many as six in one day! I love how they taste, their texture and juiciness, but most importantly, I love how they make me feel when I eat them. It's as though eating an apple is a statement of how I'm nurturing myself and how healthy I am. It feels positively virtuous.

Just as eating an apple can make you feel good about yourself, 'soul apples' are things we can do to nourish our soul. Make a list of your own soul apples. You can make the list as long as you want, but be careful to only write on it things that truly make your soul feel great! Don't be tempted to write things on your list that you think you should write. For instance, whilst writing my list, I was about to write 'swimming in the cool, azure sea' but then I hesitated. Actually, I'm not a lover of the sea, at least not to swim in. I love to look at it, to listen to it and smell it in the air - but from the safety of the beach or (better still) a beach bar, whilst sipping a pink gin and tonic. Now we're talking! You'll know it in your heart if the soul apple is true for you.

The things on your list could include big things, like a family holiday or Christmas, but should also include smaller things that you can easily do regularly, such as reading a good book, snuggling up with your family to watch a good movie (this is one of my absolute favourites) or just having a cup of coffee at the kitchen table. It's a good idea to include things you can do alone, as well as with others. Add to it as often as you want to, as new interests enter your life.

You will probably want to delete some things from the list too - remember, as you change and develop, you are likely to find that some things you used to enjoy just don't do it for you anymore. I looked at my list of soul apples recently and allowed myself a self-indulgent smile, as I realised that so many of the things I used to enjoy doing, just seem a bit empty now; instead, I have a whole new heap of mind apples to add to the list! It's a great way of confirming how you are changing and developing as a person.

Finally, and most importantly, make sure you take time to enjoy your soul apples regularly. This really needs to be a priority in your life – just as it is so important to nourish our bodies regularly, it is equally important to nourish our souls. I promise you'll thank me for it.

READ WITHOUT READING

My life is busy. I have a family (including a dog) and a home to take care of, as well as my career, and I simply don't have a spare hour or two each day that I can set aside to curl up with a book – as much as I would dearly love to do that (it is, of course one of my 'soul apples'!) We all know that as well as being therapeutic, reading is such a powerful way to learn and improve who we are and make positive changes in our lives. By learning from other people who have discovered useful strategies to improve their lives, I feel I have fast-tracked my own self-improvement. I do, therefore, make sure I find some time to read each week, but I am so grateful to have discovered an infinite supply of wisdom available through YouTube videos and audio books.

Many of the books I have read are available to listen to by downloading them, or listening to them on YouTube. This has been a life-changing discovery for me. Now, I listen to inspiring YouTube clips whilst I am getting ready for work, getting ready for bed, driving (just ensure the content of the clip doesn't involve deep relaxation or meditation, as this could be positively dangerous!) and I even enjoy doing the ironing and cleaning the bathroom nowadays, as it is a great excuse to listen to more powerful ideas!

Many people, my own husband included, say they don't like to read or can't find the time and I totally empathise with this. Years went by when I hardly picked up a book, except when I was on holiday and then I only read trashy novels that I came to realise were totally unfulfilling - more about escaping my reality than trying to improve it. I have always been a fan of multi-tasking. Yes, I know that all the best advice tells us to focus on completing one thing before moving on to the next, but I've never got my head round this and still struggle with it. However, I don't think it could be disputed that listening to some high-quality self-improvement material whilst putting on my makeup is at all detrimental to my time management. In fact, I swear the uplifting, motivating voice of the reader actually makes me apply my makeup even faster! Win, win! So, go ahead and listen to some motivating material whilst going about your daily tasks. It even makes doing the dusting fun! YouTube is really clever in that it selects new audio and video clips based on your past selections, so it follows your natural interests and leads you to new, but related, ideas. Because of this, I have been led to discover many new mentors, each giving their own individual (yet reassuringly similar) advice, who I had previously not heard of. Here are a few of my favourites to get you started: Marisa Peer, Steven Kotler, Vishen Lakhiani, Tim Ferriss, Tony Robbins, Shawn Achor, Jeff Olson, Dawson Church, Joe Dispenza ... I could go on!

'FEEL THE FEAR AND DO IT ANYWAY!'

Ok, so you've heard of the book by Susan Jeffers, and maybe you've read it. If you have, you can skip this bit, but you'll hopefully find it a really useful recap, and if you haven't already read it – keep reading!

It's so important for our self-esteem and wellbeing that we don't just stick to what we know and feel comfortable with, day in and day out. The fact is, doing something a bit scary makes us feel amazing afterwards, because we get that rush of adrenaline as well as that sense of achievement and pride that spurs us on to accomplish more. If we don't push ourselves, we become even more scared of what is not familiar to us. Now, I'm not talking about climbing mountains (unless, that's what floats your boat, of course, in which case, get those hiking boots on), but about doing something which takes you outside of your comfort zone – even if it's only just outside. You'll find that your comfort zone then expands and that thing that seemed scary, suddenly doesn't feel so scary anymore and you start to wonder what else you could achieve. There is little as sad as a life wasted because people are too scared to do the things they truly want to do. I've seen people do it and it breaks my heart, which was my main motivation for writing this book in the first place.

To expand the problem even more, some people are even too scared to admit that they're scared and pretend, even to themselves, that they are fine just doing what they are doing, thank you very much indeed, and that they don't feel the need to push themselves further than their daily lives push them. But, in response to that, I can't help but wonder – how much better could your life be if you knew, without any shadow of a doubt, that you could do anything you desired and you were guaranteed to be successful. Changes the perspective on things a bit, doesn't it? Ask yourself that question now and write a list of anything that springs to mind, no matter how far-fetched those things may seem. If you were guaranteed to be successful, how would it feel to be doing those things and, in your later years, to look back at your life and proclaim that you have achieved them? Probably pretty exciting and empowering! Well then, if the only thing stopping you is your fear, is it really worth avoiding doing them? Remember, you control your feelings, your feelings don't control you, so choose to feel the fear and do it anyway!

To start with, choose something from your list that doesn't overwhelm you, something that you don't look at and think 'No way could I ever do that!' Choose something that seems 'doable'. Or even something that you could make a step towards achieving by doing a small thing. Big goals can usually be broken down into smaller ones and by following these, one by one, we manage to achieve the big one at the end. In the introduction, I explained how if we were able to wake up in the morning and see the whole day ahead of us and what it would entail, it may overwhelm us to the point that we would happily stay in bed. In the same way, big goals may overwhelm us and seem so unattainable that we avoid them completely. So, choose a goal from your list and break it down into the steps you would need to take to complete it.

I can draw on my own experience of this, using the example of writing this book. Many people dream about writing a book in their lifetime - and few actually do it. Yes, it did feel overwhelming to me, too, and out of reach. I told myself I didn't have time and that I wasn't a good enough writer and that nobody would want to read it and that if I wrote it and nobody read it, it would be a total waste of the time I did have, which was already so limited ... What a doubter I was! I could have just given up there and then, accepted that I just didn't have it in me to make it happen and carry on with my life as it was. But, fortunately, I am too stubborn/determined/curious/adventurous - whatever the reason, I just did it.

I broke down my ultimate goal of writing a book into smaller steps by deciding to write a little each week and not putting pressure on myself to do it by a certain date or producing a particular word count. I decided to put myself in the frame of mind that I was enjoying writing, just for the sake of doing it. And I was! I was surprised by how easy it was to write and how much pleasure I got from it - the words just seemed to flow. I think it's because I was writing from the heart and everything I wrote felt genuine. I also imagined somebody (just one person - perhaps it was you!) reading my book and smiling, and thinking that it had helped them in some way. Before I knew it, I had enough words to create this book and after doing some research about how to turn my words into a published book (another step that was far easier than I imagined) my dream was suddenly my reality!

The thing that scares me the most is remembering all those times I thought about writing the book and then told myself that it was just a silly dream and it would never work, which made me put the idea to the back of my mind. I am so grateful that, somehow, I decided to ignore my negative self and believe in my positive self, otherwise this book would never have been written. Picture yourself in ten, twenty, thirty years time. Do you want to look back with regret that you didn't even try to achieve your dream? Or, how will you feel looking back, knowing that you achieved it? It's a no-brainer!

MAKE THE
UNEXCITING EXCITING

Come on, admit it, don't we all want a bit more excitement in our lives? What if we could feel a bit more of that every day, just by doing things slightly differently?

Something you should know about me is that I hate being bored! In fact, I'd rather be rushed off my feet, my head buzzing with all the things I need to do than have nothing to do. I obviously love having my down time too, but the thought of sitting in front of the TV every evening, aimlessly switching channels, trying to find something to entertain me, is repellant to me. I just love to be busy and productive most of the time - my down time feels so much sweeter! However, sometimes I feel I just don't have the time or energy to do 'more', so I just choose to do 'different'.

We all tend to stick to our own routines (and if you have children, your life almost depends on it) but it can get in the way of freeing up our minds to alternative ways of doing and thinking about things. If we don't evaluate and change things sometimes, we can end up stuck in a rut - BORING! To cure this, I have a saying that I often put into practice: 'Jooj it up!'

(By the way, it's <u>really</u> important to know how to pronounce 'jooj', as the pronunciation is essential to convey the true meaning of the word: both the letters 'j' are pronounced as they would be in the French language. Think of the 'J' in Jean-Claude Van Damme. Got that? Please do not attempt to pronounce 'jooj' as it looks like it would be pronounced in English - yuck!)

Anyway, the essence of 'joojing' something up is simply to make it better or more exciting and it can be applied to almost anything. For instance, could you travel to work along a slightly different route? Could you try doing your weekly shop in a different store? Could you try a new recipe for dinner? These are just basic things that can easily be done, but which can make our lives just that bit more interesting - and maybe the lives of others around us, too.

Try making a list (yes, another list) of the things you do on a regular basis which can be quite mundane (such as shopping, driving the kids to school, cooking dinner) and think about how you could 'jooj them up. Doing new things makes us feel more alive and open to trying more new things – and who knows where this may lead!

DRESS YOUR BEST

When we put on our best clothes and do our hair, we tend to feel good about ourselves. That's why we dress up for special occasions – because we want to feel our best and feel like we look our best. But why save feeling great for those special occasions? Why not feel great every day? I don't mean we should dress as though we're going to a wedding every day (although, if you want to, I'm not judging), but taking a pride in our appearance helps us to feel more confident and hence, happier. I aim to feel good everywhere I go and whilst this means dressing appropriately for the occasion (I really wouldn't wear a tiara to go shopping), I take a bit of time to choose my clothes thoughtfully and do my make-up and hair so I leave the house feeling good about myself. This may simply mean wearing my favourite jeans and shirt if I'm going shopping or out for lunch, or a dress and heels for a party.

I absolutely love heels! I often wear them with jeans, too - just to 'jooj' up my outfit. I know there are many women who hate wearing heels because, yes, they can be uncomfortable, and who wants to be afraid to walk down the street in case they stumble or trip? I used to feel like that and would always go for comfort over appearance, but I am very proud to say that I've managed to master my heels! I can even run in them now! Well, when I say 'run', it is a term I use very loosely and I'm sure those of you are 'proper' runners would laugh at me for calling it 'running' at all. Oh, how I envy you! But the truth is that I can 'run' almost as well in my heels as I can 'run' in my trainers and that's justification enough for me that heels are ok.There is something about the 'clip-clop' sound they make that I find weirdly satisfying, rather like the 'tip-tap' sound of the keyboard as I am writing this book. Maybe I have sensory issues - it seems likely - but I'm not going to explore that now. I'm just going to take the pleasure from it unquestioningly. As Sheryl Crow sings: 'If it makes you happy, it can't be that bad.' I'm going with that.

Please note, I am not advocating here that everyone should wear heels. What I'm saying is that you should wear whatever makes you feel a bit more special, and enjoy the feeling this brings. For me, it's often heels - and sometimes colourful flip-flops, sometimes trainers ... like I said, it depends on the occasion. I just like to spend a bit of time thinking about what I'm going to feel my best in that day.

Having said all that, I must confess, I don't spend much time or money getting my hair done - in fact I am quite lazy when it comes to getting a trim. This seems especially ludicrous because my sister-in-law is a talented hairdresser who owns her own salon, and I know I am welcome to pop into the salon whenever I want to! Instead, I tend to wait for her to remind me to come and get my hair done. I'm sure she looks at me with despair and, being as polite as she is, waits until she can't bear to look at me any more, so kindly suggests that I come and get my hair cut - she is so diplomatic. But I do always make sure I style my hair before going out to face the world. I'm also a bit lazy when it comes to make-up; I don't wear a lot of make-up and it doesn't take me much time at all to apply it (sadly, I'm not fortunate enough to have another sister-in-law who is a make-up artist), but I do always make sure I feel like I look ok before I walk out of the door.

In summary, it's not really about how amazing my hair, make-up or clothes look, and it's definitely not about how much money I've spent on them! I'm not trying to draw attention to myself by looking drop-dead gorgeous (a little voice inside my head is laughing right now at this possibility - oh, the subconscious mind can be so cruel!) It's about feeling I've made a bit of an effort, that I'm worthy of giving myself that little bit of time and attention, that makes me walk that little bit taller and smile that little bit wider. People do seem to smile at me more nowadays (maybe because I'm smiling more myself) and I am more likely to strike up conversations with people I don't know - another great happiness booster!

YOUR IDEAL SELF

If you were the perfect version of yourself, what would that look like? What would you feel like? How would you behave? What kinds of thoughts would you have and what kinds of things would you say?

Spend a bit of time visualising this and tell yourself, 'I have the power within me to be that person.' If you do this every day, you will actually get closer to being that person - I promise, it works! No, you're not likely to change overnight (although you will probably find that some aspects of the 'new you' will appear quite quickly), but over time, if you keep focussing on who you want to be, you will gradually become that person, and all the while you will stay motivated to keep changing because you notice those small changes occurring. And if you can make small changes happen, you can make bigger changes happen. In fact, lots of small changes in themselves make a bigger change - it's like putting in place smaller pieces of a larger jigsaw.

Here's another expression that I use: 'Believe it – achieve it!" So, as well as visualising the perfect you, it is important to tell yourself that 'it will happen,' and believe it! This may be difficult at first, because you are so used to seeing yourself as you currently are, and because your not-so-positive habits are controlled by your subconscious mind, it can make you feel like this is just who you are and that there's no point trying to change it. But that is so untrue! You can re-train your subconscious mind and replace those unwanted habits with new ones that will make you become who you want to be. And a very effective way of re-training your subconscious mind is through repetition, repetition, repetition -

until your new thoughts become part of your subconscious reality.

I found believing that I could change a bit tricky at first, so don't get too hung up on it. Just go with it - keep visualising and you will see that things are changing which will prove to yourself that you can believe it - and so the cycle continues. Once I'd seen a few small changes, I began to wonder 'What if I really do have the power within me to change' and once I'd put it out there as a possibility, more things started to change, which was just so exciting! I began to see my future as a whole new set of possibilities, rather than the limited way I'd lived my life previously.

It will soon seem perfectly natural to you to see yourself as your best self, and without realising it, you will gradually become more and more like that person you aspire to be. Make sure you take the time to recognise and celebrate these changes as they occur, as this will spur you on to make even more changes for the better. The sky's the limit - and that is such an empowering thought!

To help you to visualise your ideal future self, you could begin by simply creating a mental image of yourself looking really happy! Exaggerate the image as much as you can by seeing yourself in an ecstatic pose, for instance leaping into the air with a huge smile on your face. Feel free to ensure your hair/clothes/make-up are absolutely perfect. You could even drop/gain a few pounds – anything you want! Just make sure the image is really positive so that when you see it in your mind, it makes you feel really good about yourself. Practise seeing the image by bringing it to mind at least once every day and notice how happy it makes you feel. This image then serves as an instant happiness booster whenever you need one. The more you recall the image and the more vivid you make it, and the intensity of the feeling of happiness that accompanies it, the easier it will be for it to empower you to feel happy whenever you need to, and the sooner your dreams will come true!

FIND THE HUMOUR (SHUT YOUR PIE HOLE!)

I absolutely love this strategy to feel happier and it has been the cause of much hilarity in several situations. It's a great tension-reliever and can be used anywhere - but please read on and take note of the caution below!

Think of a funny expression that you can use whenever things are getting a bit much and you need to let off a little steam – something to just take the edge off when a situation threatens to become stressful and zap your happiness. My favourite is "Shut your pie hole!" This came from the film Paddington and, for some reason, it just tickled me. One day shortly afterwards, my husband and I were in the kitchen and he was moaning about something (at least, to my ears, he was moaning – I think he thought we were 'discussing') and I suddenly got the urge to tell him to shut up. Now, had I have followed that instinct, it would undoubtedly have caused a full-blown argument. So, I had a quick rethink and called out in my best Scottish accent (as Mrs Bird does in the film) "Oh, shut your pie hole!" This not only broke the tension but went one step further - it made us both laugh. We all know it's not possible to have an argument if both people involved are laughing. I can't remember whether we actually resolved the issue that he had been moaning about (I mean, that we had been 'discussing'), but it certainly helped to avoid the argument that would have erupted had I gone with my 'shut up' option.

I'm not afraid to admit (in fact, I'm quite proud of it) that I've tried this strategy at work, too, when someone has been bleating on about new policies and practices which appear to me utterly pointless - although I must say that I have never said "Shut your pie hole" out loud. I am not that unprofessional - however tempting it might have been! I simply shout it loudly in my head, and it never fails to lighten my mood.

Now for the caution: I must warn you, sometimes it can lighten the load a little too much, and I have almost sniggered in the middle of a serious discussion at work, which would have been very unprofessional indeed! So, my advice to you is to use "Shut your pie hole" (or whichever phrase you choose to use) wisely - but make sure you enjoy it!

CHOOSE HAPPY!

If only it we had a 'happy' button that we could just press - and then just feel happy! Wouldn't that be great, to be able to turn on our happiness as if flipping a switch? What an absurd idea. Or is it? Remember, we control our emotions, they do not control us. So, why does it seem impossible to change our emotions at will? Are we really in control? Yes we are, but it certainly doesn't feel like it, does it?

If we really are in control of our feelings (and logically, why wouldn't we be - they come from within us), then it makes sense that we can change them if we want to. But what makes this seem impossible is that it is largely our subconscious mind that controls them, not our conscious mind. If it were our conscious mind in control, we could simply become aware of how we are feeling, consider how we want to feel instead and just choose to replace the horrible feeling with the nice one. Simple! But our subconscious mind is far more tricky than that. It doesn't respond to simple instructions like our conscious mind does. To change our subconscious mind, we need to be one step ahead in order to retrain it - and this is totally possible. The subconscious mind is essentially a set of habits (thoughts, feelings, actions) that we have generated through years of our life experiences, and which ultimately serves to protect us from perceived dangers and keep us alive. I say 'perceived' because, often, the 'dangers' are not really dangerous at all, and avoiding these 'dangers' can actually hold us back from being who we really want to be.

The language of the subconscious mind is senses and emotions - not spoken or written language like that of the conscious mind.

If we experience something upsetting or frightening, our subconscious mind stores this experience and tries to avoid us being in that situation again by making sure we avoid it in the future. Remember, it's all about that outdated caveman instinct for survival and so many situations that our subconscious mind encourages us to avoid are unnecessary and even detrimental to avoid. The scary thing is, we don't even know that it's happening - it's all going on behind the scenes whilst we get on with our lives. If we could only connect with our subconscious mind and tell it, in language that it understands, not to react in this way to those 'dangers', it would stop. Well, the great news is, we can! There are different ways that we can reprogram our subconscious minds; hypnosis is one way, although this can be expensive and many people feel uncomfortable putting themselves in the hands of a stranger in this way, or maybe don't believe it will even work; meditation is another, although many people find it difficult to relax enough to do this. But there is another way that you can do all by yourself that won't cost you a bean and that I have already mentioned - repetition, repetition, repetition.

If we jump every time we see a spider because one of our parents were frightened of spiders when we were a child, and that is the 'reality' that has been programmed into our subconscious mind, we will continue to be afraid of spiders until we change that belief. I have done this myself. I used to be terrified of spiders (probably because my dad was, and still is) until I simply decided I didn't want to be any more. I'd discovered through my reading that the only two fears we are born with are the fear of falling (very sensible) and the fear of loud noises (maybe not so important to us these days) and that every other fear is learned by us through our experiences - and often by watching others experience their fears, especially our parents, and believing they are real. So, I reasoned, that if our fears are learned behaviours, we can surely unlearn them - and now I know we can! No, it doesn't happen overnight. I didn't wake up one day with a love for spiders and I still wouldn't pick one up in my hands by choice. But I just kept telling myself that I wasn't afraid of them - and more importantly, I allowed myself to believe this - and after a while, it was my new reality.

So, it stands to reason that if we can eliminate a fear by talking ourself out of it as I did, we can surely talk ourself into feeling happy. Again, it is not something that we can do overnight, but with practice and belief, we can do it. I have done it! By being conscious of negative feelings and repeatedly telling myself that they are not wanted and replacing them with positive ones, I have become a much happier person. And I don't even need to think about it any more - my subconscious mind has taken over and it's now a natural state for me to choose to be happy, rather than to feel sad, angry or worried. Sounds too good to be true? Of course, there are times that I do feel angry (the dirty cups in the bedroom spring to mind again here) and sad, and even worried, but those feelings are far less frequent in my life now, whereas they were certainly my default setting a couple of years ago. My default setting is now happy, because I've reprogrammed my subconscious mind that that is how I want to feel, and my subconscious mind has caught on, realising that it is safe for me to feel happy for the majority of the time. Being happy hasn't caused me to be eaten by a tiger, to be abandoned by my social group and left to die alone or to fall down a huge hole and die in agonising pain. And the happier I am, the happier I get! And the happier I get, the more powerful I feel - the more control I feel I have over my emotions, my choices and my life. That's the power of happy!

Have a try - just choose to be happy! Use your conscious mind to notice when you're feeling anxious/angry/sad and tell yourself that you are choosing to be happy instead. Keep repeating this and you will reprogram your subconscious mind until being happy is your default setting, too.

A proviso: I'm not saying that you should be happy 100% of the time - I'm certainly not jumping for joy from the moment I awake until the moment I fall asleep. Negative emotions are ultimately a warning sign that we need to fix something. So, when I feel down, I ask myself why I'm feeling like that and try to work out what my subconscious is telling me - what the perceived danger is. Sometimes, those feelings will be a prompt for us to take action to fix a problem and then we can get back to feeling happy again - job done! However, sometimes, our over-protective subconscious mind anticipates potential 'danger' where there really is none. Once you've recognised this, you can assure yourself that you are still safe and get back to being happy again!

COFFEE FOR CONFIDENCE

I've never been a drug-taker (I just thought I'd throw that out there, in case you were wondering) but during the last couple of years, I have developed a passion for coffee. I love the taste, and even more, I love the effect it has on me. I find it gives me a lovely buzz and fills my head with positive ideas and impulses. I do my best work after a cup of coffee and, at times, I'm sure I could solve any problem I was faced with: I feel kind of invincible! This led me to the phrase 'coffee for confidence'. (I also found that tea does a similar thing, although I'm not as keen on the taste of tea.)

Now, as I'm sure you've already worked out, I'm a great believer in the power of the mind being able to influence how we think and feel and if we truly believe something, then our subconscious mind makes it become true for us - so maybe my feelings of invincibility are due to my conscious mind telling my subconscious mind that the coffee actually does turn me into Superwoman for a while. Quite frankly, I don't care whether the effect is real or imagined, or a bit of both – it works for me, so I'm going with it!

A while after I'd discovered the power of coffee for me personally, I was sent a daily update from Mindvalley (created by the amazing Vishen Lakhiani) raving about the positive effects of coffee on the brain! Vishen describes coffee as 'the closest thing to a Marvel Comics-style Super Serum that scientists have ever discovered.' I knew it! Vishen claims that drinking coffee makes you smarter, makes you live longer and helps you maintain a healthy weight. Result! You can find the clip by visiting blog.mindvalley.com. Of course, you need to use some common sense here and not overdo it, or it can cause sleep problems and anxiety (yes, I know this from personal experience and it's not nice) so try not to drink it too late in the day (I avoid it after 2pm and sleep like a baby) or drink too many cups within too short a period of time (to avoid those shakes and the urge to run round the block a few times). Otherwise - enjoy!

WHAT IF ...?

This is one of my favourite exercises and it has amazing power! I simply ask myself "What if ...?" and imagine something I'd really love in my life. For example, "What if I had the perfect job that I loved doing every day?", "What if I woke up every day feeling positive?", "What if I spent more time making fabulous memories with my family?"

When we ask ourselves these questions, our subconscious mind responds by considering ways to actually make those things happen; so, gradually, we become closer and closer to those 'what ifs' becoming our reality. I can honestly say that so many things have come true for me by doing this exercise, and I can see the progress I am making in those that haven't yet - I know they are definitely on their way!

I have a rule when I do this exercise that I am not allowed to consider reasons why the 'what if ...?' might not work - if I did, I could just talk myself out of it, because we can always think of many reasons why we can't have what we want, and then our subconscious mind would accept that as our reality and prevent it from happening. I love to fantasise about what life would be like if I had those things I wanted. Pure fantasy, like a child playing make-believe. It's such a wonderful thing to do and makes me feel so excited, knowing that I am making even more improvements in my life. You know what I'm going to say next, don't you: believing those things will come true will make them happen even faster!

I have recently asked myself another question: "Why not?" We often tell ourselves we can't do or have something as it seems out of our reach, but does it have to be? Why can't I leave my job and start up my own company? Why can't I learn to tap dance? Why can't I write a book? The answer to all of these questions is simply: I am not allowing myself to let these things happen! If I'm the only reason these things might not happen, it stands to reason that if I just get out of the way, I can allow them to. All of these things are totally possible, if only we give ourselves the power to visualise and realise them.

We've started doing the 'what if ...?' exercise as a family, too, often at the dinner table - and we follow the same rule where we are not allowed to give any thought to why these things might not being possible, because we choose to believe that anything is possible. It has opened several doors of possibility for us as a family, and many others are sure to be opened in the near and distant future! I love how it teaches our children to be open-minded and consider all the possibilities there are for them in this world. After all, isn't that what life is - a plethora of possibilities from which we choose which ones to make our reality?

PROBLEMS OR OPPORTUNITIES?

There are two main ways that we grow – through moments of enlightenment, where we suddenly get an idea through some inspiration, or through the challenges we face in life. Michael Beckwith calls these 'Satori' and 'Kensho'. The second is the most common, and if we look carefully at these challenges we are faced with, and try to find the lessons within them, we can grow at a quicker pace.

I know I must get on my family's nerves at times (maybe more often that I'd care to admit) because I'm sure they see me as being on some weird mission to be the happiest person on Earth, as I'm always looking for the good in everything. Sometimes, I sense they just want to have a good old moan about their day (such as is the conditioning of human nature) but I simply won't have it - not on my watch! Of course, I never belittle their concerns or worries, but I do encourage them to see that problems are valuable opportunities to grow. My stock phrase when they share such concerns with me is: 'Hmmm, so what can you learn from this that will help you to grow?' This puts the ball squarely back into their court, encouraging them to take responsibility for choosing how to react. Not that I'm implying the problem is their fault (although sometimes it is - they are human, after all) but that it is their responsibility to find a way to overcome and learn from it. I often remind them that they cannot change the way other people behave, but they can change the way they react to other people and this is no one else's responsibility except their own. Yes, I really do think I get on their nerves! I don't want them to become 'victims', where all they can see is how unfair the world is and how powerless they are to do anything about it except moan. I do hate moaning! My heart lights up when I hear one of them using one of my phrases - I know they get it! Of course, it's far easier to be the coach than it is to be coached, but through coaching each other, it shows their understanding of the concept and how they are strengthening it within themselves - after all, one of the best ways to master a skill is to teach it to someone else.

We naturally tend to look at the negative aspects when faced with difficulties in our lives (the survival instinct strikes again) but rephrasing in a positive way and searching for the opportunities for change and growth that could come from the situation, will not only help you to manage the situation better, by feeling you are more in control of how it is affecting you, but it will help you to deal with similar situations better in the future. Even if the only positive you can find is becoming more resilient, then that is great! So think deeply and ask: "How can I become a better person through this experience? How could this experience help me in the future? How could this experience help me to help others?" It won't take away the pain of the situation but it will help you to accept it and reduce the "why me?" reaction that we tend to feel.

Similarly, looking back at past experiences in your life that have been difficult can help you to overcome present difficulties. Consider a time in your life that was particularly difficult and consider what you did to overcome it. What thoughts helped you? Did anyone else help you? Remember, you don't need to go it alone – think of the human race as being a huge support network – you just need to tap into it.

JUST DO IT!

I was talking to my twelve-year-old daughter recently, and sharing with her how I had to do a particular task that I didn't want to do, and that I'd been reading about how to become motivated and to stop procrastinating by focussing on the end results rather than the task itself. I was quite pleased with my new discovery and decided to put it into practice. Whilst I was talking to my daughter, she sat, listening patiently as she always does, and when I'd finished speaking, she looked at me and said, "Mum, do you know the best way to get a job done that you don't want to do?" I looked at her quizzically and asked her to tell me. "Just do it!" she cried. I looked at her admiringly – such wisdom for a twelve-year-old. Of course, she was absolutely right.

I'm a thinker and a planner. In fact, I'm an over-thinker and an over-planner and my darling daughter had made me suddenly realise that by contemplating what I needed to do, visualising the optimum end result and planning how I was going to make it all come together, I was outrageously over-thinking the whole process and making it outrageously complicated. It made me think about how I plan to do virtually everything that I do in my life, and through this planning I put myself under such pressure that I'm exhausted before I've even started. Yes, I'm also a perfectionist. My amazing daughter went on to describe how if she has to do a task that she doesn't want to do – such as the dreaded bedroom tidy, including removing the dirty cups – she doesn't think about it, she doesn't plan what she needs to do first, what equipment she might need, or even when she is going to do it; she just does it! Simple!

Since this enlightenment, I have applied this philosophy to all sorts of areas of my life and have found it to be so useful! It's like being given the key to my freedom! It has made me realise how much time I wasted thinking about and planning a task and how much energy this took from me - and how grouchy it made me! Needless to say, my family are much happier with the more happy-go-lucky me that I now am.

I've even taken it a step further and applied it to making decisions. As an over-thinker and over-planner, I used to consider the multitude of possible outcomes of decisions I needed to make, and would more often than not err on the side of caution and decide against doing something that could have been a powerful life experience – or may have just been fun! Since I've adopted the 'just do it' approach, we have much more fun and I'm probably a much nicer person to be around, because I don't over-analyse every little thing.

Please don't misunderstand me here, I'm not saying that I throw caution to the wind and allow my children to roam free, causing havoc whilst I smile proudly at their developing life-skills. I'm still a very responsible mummy, but I've decided to just let the small things go and if things do go wrong, we learn from them.

DO SOMETHING - ANYTHING!

Are you a procrastinator? Do you put off starting things because you're not sure how to get started, don't feel ready to commit to completing the whole project or the time just doesn't 'feel right'? Welcome to the club! I've been doing some research about perfectionism recently - because I realised it was holding me back in lots of ways. (Needless to say, everyone around me breathed a huge sigh of relief, and they seem much happier now that I am working on it!)

Through my research, I have discovered that procrastination is a major factor in perfectionism. Please forgive my ignorance, but until I looked into it properly, I had always believed that procrastination was only for lazy people. The word 'procrastination' conjured up images of scruffy people siting about on their sofas watching crap TV and not bothering to tidy or clean their houses. How awfully judgmental of me! Now I understand what it really is and why it happens, I've realised that I'm one of the biggest procrastinators going! (For the record, my house is generally clean and tidy because that's another symptom of my perfectionism, and I never spend the day on the sofa just watching crap TV, because I feel that would just destroy me. As I said, I am working on my perfectionism, I haven't conquered it yet!)

One of the main reasons we procrastinate is because, at the beginning of a task, it's often difficult to see how it will all turn out. We don't know whether we will be successful or not, we don't know how difficult or time-consuming the task will be, and if we already have pretty busy lives - and let's face it, who hasn't? - it is so much easier to stay busy doing those routine tasks that we are more predictable and we know will turn out ok. For example, If I suddenly found myself with a spare hour in my day, would I decide to start that gardening project I'd been thinking about, or start to write the first chapter of the new book I've planned, or would I use it to make sure the house was tidy, the dinner was prepared and the laundry was done? Of course, I'd sort out the house, the dinner and the laundry. Every time! Why? Because they're easy to do, they take little effort and my ego can congratulate itself on a job well done. Instant gratification! Conversely, getting part way through a project feels risky - it puts us under pressure to complete it and, for a perfectionist like me, it can play on my mind, causing stress and anxiety. I often hear that little voice in my head admonishing me to 'just finish the job' and I know there is a part of me that worries that I may never get it finished which would then make me a complete failure. Extreme, I know, but that is the nature of perfectionism!

In order to reduce my procrastinating tendencies, I've had to have a strong word with myself and give myself permission to leave a task uncompleted. Yes, it was really difficult at first and I felt like I was putting myself up for criticism from everybody else as I imagined their responses to my 'laziness': "Why haven't you finished it? Why did you start it in the first place? It looks even worse now!" I've had to remind myself that I'm not Magnus Magnusson from Mastermind ("I've started, so I'll finish.") and it is ok to start a project and leave it midway - in fact, sometimes it is even necessary. And, actually, nobody has criticised me at all. I have found that if I schedule when I'm going to take on the next part of the project, it makes me feel better. I know I won't just keep looking at the unfinished project and wishing I hadn't started because I don't know when I'll get it finished. In fact, it might take me several attempts to get the task done and that's fine, too.

The hardest part of tackling a large or unwanted project is just making a start. As I've mentioned before, it is easy to overthink and overplan and not get round to actually doing the job. So, when the voice in my head says "I really should sort out that front flowerbed - it looks like a jungle! But I can really only spare half an hour at the moment, so I think I'll just leave it for now", there is another voice which now says, even louder, "Do something - anything!" I now find that just making a start gives me enough motivation and inspiration to keep going, even if the job is done in small slots of time and takes me a while to get it completed. The other benefit of working in this way is that, the chances are, some kind helpful person will see that you have made a start on the project and will offer to help you to complete it! Now that's not a bad consequence for being less of a procrastinator!

TALLY SMALL SUCCESSES

Closely related to 'Do something - anything!", a strategy to avoid procrastinating, I have devised a points system which really helps me to chunk down any task and feel proud of my achievements (so inspiring me to carry on), rather than to feel disappointed that I haven't completed the whole task (so making me want to forget the whole thing and give up). I give myself a point for each part of the task I have completed. Yes, I actually write these points down as tallies on a piece of paper so I can visually see my achievements.

As I have already explained, when you a perfectionist, it is really difficult not to want to do everything at once and do it perfectly. Of course, we all know that's impossible, but just try telling your inner voice that when she is screaming at you that you're a failure! So, if I was tidying my son's wardrobe, I might give myself a point for just opening the doors and having a look inside (even small successes are successes), a couple of points for taking out all the clothes from the hanging rail which are too small/stained/have holes in/are otherwise unsuitable, another two points for doing the same with one of the drawers etc. It really doesn't matter how many points you give yourself, but the act of rewarding yourself for doing something - anything! - makes you feel like you are achieving and focuses your attention on what you have done and not what you haven't.

However, one word of warning for those of you who are a certified perfectionists: do not let this point system make you compete with yourself to improve your score tomorrow! Just imagine, you wake up thinking, 'I scored 25 points sorting out that wardrobe yesterday - I bet I can score 30 sorting out the kitchen cupboards today!' Suddenly, you're under pressure to achieve and that's not the idea here. Of course, it is good (and necessary) to have goals and plans of things we want to do each day, but if we allow them to put us under tremendous pressure, the joy is taken away. Remember the whole idea of the points system is that it is supposed to be fun and motivating!

THE SOUNDTRACK
TO YOUR LIFE

I'm sure you'll understand how listening to a piece of music can change your mood. It can take us back to a particular time in our lives when it was one of our favourite tunes, or to when it was playing at a special event. When I was younger and my first child was just eight months old, one of the babies in the baby group I belonged to, tragically died. It was devastating. We went to the funeral to support our friend and during the service, they played Michael Jackson's 'You Are Not Alone'. That was many years ago, but I still cannot listen to that song without wanting to sob.

Thankfully, music can also have the opposite effect. I'm sure you could name, right now, a song that makes you feel happy, a song that makes you feel calm, one that makes you feel sad etc. So, to tap into that, I use music to help me to create my mood. This has been especially effective when I am finding a task difficult to do and need to find some motivation to keep going. I have found that the best type of music to listen to when I am stuck with a task needing lots of brain power, is uplifting classical. It has no words, so I am not tempted to sing along and become distracted (yes, I love a good sing-song and I often analyse the words of songs for their meaning - not very useful when I have an important report to write.)

In fact, I have now built up a repertoire of songs as an accompaniment to the different areas of my life. It is like I have my own soundtrack, so if they ever make a musical about me, it will be easy for the musical composer! I have songs and artists that accompany me when I am cooking, ironing, doing the housework, driving the kids to school, being on holiday - virtually everything. Luckily, my family tend to share my taste in music, so we're all able to share the experience together.

I also like to keep an open mind and listen out for new music and artists. This is easy with two children in the house (especially as one is a teenager) as they regularly play music by artists I've never heard of and these then often become our family soundtrack for a period of time. We subscribe to Apple Play, which allows us to download as much music as we want to for a monthly subscription; the great thing about this is that it gives you suggestions for new artists you may like based on your recent listening choices. I've discovered some fabulous artists in this way, that I may not otherwise have heard of.

Try creating your own life soundtrack of your favourite songs and artists, and build upon it as new ones enter your life. Having your own collection of songs is both soothing and uplifting and can help you to feel 'safe' when you might be feeling a bit wobbly! Having your own 'life soundtrack' also helps you to create your own identity and understand who you are and who you want to be.

START THE DAY WITH A 'MIRACLE MORNING'

I recently read Hal Elrod's book 'The Miracle Morning' (or, rather, I listened to the audiobook version over several days whilst I was doing my morning workouts) and I can honestly say that it changed my life. I guarantee there will be something in it that will change yours too. Hal talks about starting the day early, which is a scary thought to begin with and it's not until you begin having these 'Miracle Mornings' that you realise how powerful these early starts are. He gives the process the acronym SAVERS, which stands for Silence, Affirmations, Visualisation, Exercise, Reading and Scribing. Hal suggests you spend up to two hours each morning following the process, but it can be done in a much shorter time, as he later describes in the book. The process goes like this (although it can be done in any order):

Silence – just spend a few moments breathing deeply and considering the silence. Think about the things you are grateful for in your life – this never fails to put a smile on my face!

Affirmations – as I described earlier, this is spending some time telling yourself positive things about yourself that you want to come true, as though they are already true.

Visualisation – this is about visualising your perfect day, your perfect week, your perfect future and making the vision in your head so vivid that it seems as though it really is true.

Exercise – of all the books I have read or listened to (and there have been lots), not one of them has disputed the idea that exercising in the morning is a good thing. I am sure if you read the biography or autobiography on any successful leader, they will always say that exercising early in the morning is a great way to set your body and mind up for the day. And the good news is that with the realisation that HIIT (High Intensity Interval Training) can be at least as effective as longer exercise sessions, it can be done quite quickly!

Reading – Great leaders are great readers. Some have only one or two favourite books that they read over and over again for their inspiration. Some read as many as they can, picking up snippets from all different authors. Personally, I love doing this, and I often find the messages in these self-help books have huge similarities, confirming their authenticity. Remember you can listen to audio books or You Tube clips, as I've previously mentioned, rather than reading a book in print.

Scribing – I've always kept a diary during holiday times as I don't want to forget the precious moments of these special times - and because I just love writing! Hal suggests writing (scribing) a diary every day to capture those moments of clarity and learning you will get from your reading and other daily experiences. As I mentioned earlier, it is very powerful to look back at how you have developed and grown as a person, through reviewing your journal.

For full details of Hal Elrod's Miracle Morning, check out his book, as well as his newer publication The Miracle Equation. I promise you'll be glad you did!

FORGIVE

Forgiving others for the wrongs we perceive they have done to us, can be incredibly difficult. Well-meaning friends and family members can make the situation worse by telling us we "must be so angry" with that person, or for exclaiming "How could he/she do this to you?" We may even feel obliged to be angry at someone for fear of seeming weak if we don't vow to avenge the wrong-doer. Forgiveness is particularly difficult if the person who wronged us is someone we love - it is far easier to forgive someone who has wronged us if they don't mean much to us or we'll never see them again. We all know someone (perhaps that person is you) who harbours a grudge against somebody and who takes every opportunity to rant about that person. What a waste of energy and what a wasted opportunity to feel happy instead!

What if we reframe how we think of the situation? What if we think of it in terms of how it makes us feel, rather than what the person has done? When we harbour grudges, we replay what that person did to us and focus on their 'evil intentions'. We think about what they did and why they did it and assume they meant to hurt us. The more we focus on that, the angrier we get. What if we focussed on our own feelings and intentions instead? Do we really want to spend our time being upset/annoyed/bitter? Wouldn't we much rather feel happy and contented instead? Of course we would! We just need to let it go - it worked for Elsa in the Disney movie Frozen and she had a whole load of baggage to deal with! We really can choose to do this if we want to. Remember, we control our thoughts, our thoughts do not control us. We just need to take that control and choose to forgive.

A tool that can help us to forgive, is attempting to understand. We might never understand why a person has behaved in a certain way, but just trying to see things from their point of view will go a long way to getting us to the point of forgiveness. In Hal Elrod's book The Miracle Equation, he suggests that we look at it this way: if we had grown up as that person, living the experiences that they have lived and being in the situations that they have been in, we would very likely have behaved in exactly the same way.

The reason we get annoyed with the apparent misdemeanours of others is because we see things from our own point of view, not theirs - from the point of view of our own reality, which has been created by our own experiences, which have created our own thoughts, which have created our own beliefs. The person who wronged us behaved in that way because their beliefs led them to think that this was the right action to take. If we had that same belief system, would we not take the same actions? Of course, this is impossible to prove, and I'm not condoning bad behaviour, but I like to use this tool to try to understand the motives of others because it makes me feel better, and, ultimately, that is what I want. I can even feel sympathy, and sometimes empathy, for my perpetrator if I reframe my thinking in this way. And it is so empowering to think that I can control my thoughts enough to enable me to have a better day. As I have previously mentioned, we cannot control the actions of others, but we do have the power and responsibility to control how we react to them.

Vishen Lakhiani uses forgiveness as one of the steps in his 6-stage meditation (you can watch this on YouTube). It really is possible, we just need to want it enough! By focussing on ourselves and how we want to think and live, rather than the intentions of another towards us, we can let go of those feelings that eat us up. Rather than allowing the person who wronged us to have a continuing effect on us, we can choose not to let this happen - hugely empowering!

Note that in the first paragraph in this section, I mention forgiving others for the wrongs we 'perceive' they have done to us. I have been found guilty of jumping to conclusions and assuming that someone has wronged me intentionally, only to discover later that their intentions were totally innocent. My survival instincts at their best! My poor husband has been on the receiving end of my wrong accusations many times. Because we are each the centre of our own world and have our own thoughts, we have our own beliefs based on these thoughts - and sometimes these beliefs are not actually true! But, if we can become aware of this, we can challenge it. This isn't always easy, especially if we have held onto these beliefs for years and they have become a large part of our personal 'truth'. To change these beliefs, we need to change a part of our subconscious programming. And as you now know, this can be done, as I've described previously.

CELEBRATE!

Keeping a journal can really help you to track changes in your outlook that you may otherwise miss. We become so used to how we are 'now' and unless we monitor these changes, we may not notice that we are changing at all. Keeping a journal is a great way of recording your thoughts and feelings and can be a powerful tool in looking back to see how much you have changed. Keeping a journal also helps you to clarify your thoughts and ideas – I have often had an 'Aha!' moment whilst journaling, especially when I'm writing about something confusing or problematic. It's a bit like talking things over with yourself, without actually having to talk to yourself and feeling silly doing so! I love to look back at my previous journals to see how far I've come and it's quite enlightening and exciting when I notice that I have changed how I think, feel and react and how these reactions have now become part of who I am.

When you notice these positive changes, remember to celebrate! Congratulate yourself on becoming the new improved you. And then you can just stop trying and carry on with your life as it is. Only joking - I promise that once you realise how you have changed your life for the better, how you have become more like the person you want to be and how amazing it is to realise that you have had this power within you the whole time, you will never want to just give up and carry on as you are. You will see more possibilities for your future self - if you can change yourself as much as you already have, what else could you do? There really is no limit. I believe this is why we are here - to make ourselves the best we can possibly be and it all begins with the power of happy!

Feeling happy is not an end in itself, but the key to a world of limitless opportunities that we can not even imagine, because we have no frame of reference for it. All we know now is what we have learned so far through our life experiences. All we are now is what we have created of ourselves. Think of your life as a circle. The inside of the circle is you as you are now. The perimeter of the circle represents the possibilities you can comprehend as you are now. As you make those possibilities your new realities, the circle grows and you become a bigger 'you'. So, the perimeter of the circle also grows - more possibilities for you to make into realities. How big can the circle that is 'you' become? Well, there truly are no limits. And as you grow, so does your happiness and, along with it, your power. What an exciting future you have ahead of you and it all starts now! What are you waiting for? Grow your happiness - grow your power!

45383709R00035

Printed in Poland
by Amazon Fulfillment
Poland Sp. z o.o., Wrocław